The English Civil War

THE BEST ONE-HOUR HISTORY

Robert Freeman

The Best One-Hour History™
Kendall Lane Publishers, Palo Alto, CA
Copyright © 2014, Robert Freeman
All rights reserved.
ISBN-978-0-9892502-9-0

Contents

1 Introduction

Democracy is a fleeting commodity. After its birth in Ancient Greece and its evolution into republicanism in Ancient Rome, it disappeared from the Western world. For a thousand years after the Fall of Rome, government in Europe was a competition between the Catholic Church, local feudal lords, and weak and local kings. Around 1500, political power began to consolidate into regional monarchies—the kings in Spain, France, and England. These became the first of what we know of today as nation states. But they were not democracies.

It wasn't until the seventeenth century that democracy was reborn in the Western world. Its rebirth occurred in England as a result of the English Civil War. It was in this War that the forces of Parliament overturned the "divine right of kings." Before the century was over, England would be governed by an entirely new form of government, a constitutional monarchy. Power was shared between an executive branch (monarchy) and a legislative branch (Parliament) with a set of rules for how the country would be governed—a constitution. This book explains how that transition came about.

It begins with a discussion of the fundamental conflicts that underlay the Civil War: economic; religious; and political. It examines the rulers and events that led up to war, and then the War itself. It looks in some detail at the trial and execution of Charles I in 1649 and their implications for the balance of power in government. It analyzes the Interregnum under the rule of Oliver Cromwell when both the monarchy and the House of Lords were abolished. It quickly peruses the Restoration of monarchy in 1660 and the Glorious Revolution of 1688. It concludes with a reflection on the importance of the period and events to the founding of America.

These events were crucial to the transition in the Western World from political systems dominated by monarchy and divine right to systems centered in representation and constitutionalism. In fact, the importance of the Civil War, especially as it affected the creation of the United States and the nature of its government, is impossible to overstate. This is that story.

2 Fundamental Conflicts

There were three fundamental conflicts that underlay the English Civil War. They were economic, religious, and political. They would play back and forth on one another time and again until it was almost impossible to tell at any given time which of the forces was responsible for any given event. At some times, economic factors were paramount. At other times, religious issues ruled. And at still other times, the decisive factors were political.

Usually—though not always—these issues tended to reinforce each other, so that players on one side of the religious divide found themselves on the same side of the political and economic divides. But again, not always. It is the complex interplay between the different forces and factions that make the period so interesting and complex.

Economic Conflicts

The fundamental economic conflict was between a declining nobility (including the king) and an ascendant gentry. The nobility represented the old world, the landed aristocracy descended from feudalism and embodied in the House of Lords. The gentry represented the new world, the emerging proto-capitalists who made up the House of Commons. There were exceptions to this rule—nobles in the House of Lords who fought against the king, or gentry in the Commons who fought with him—but as a first approximation it is helpful.

The fortunes and the status of the nobility had declined markedly over the century prior to 1640. This was partly due to the deliberate policy of Tudor monarchs in the 1500s to subdue competing centers of power. They wanted a monopoly on the use of violence so that no one could challenge their rule. They were largely successful in achieving it and as a result, the nobility had less economic leverage.

For example, in 1500 there were many nobles in England who could field their own army, an undertaking requiring enormous economic resources. By 1600 there was only one. The Tudors had also confiscated Church lands after Henry VIII broke with Rome in 1535. They redistributed much of this land to aspiring gentry with the intent to build loyalty among this class and create an offset to the potentially threatening power of hostile nobles.

There were deeper economic forces at work as well. The nobility typically earned its income from rents of its lands. Rental contracts endured for years, sometimes for the life of the tenants. But the sixteenth century had seen a European-wide price inflation following the discovery of gold and silver in the new world. This meant that the effective incomes received from fixed rents had declined over time.

Merchants or commercial farmers, on the other hand, could change their prices with every transaction, every harvest, thus keeping up with inflation. And it was the rising gentry—gentlemen farmers, merchants, bankers, accountants, lawyers, etc.—who claimed the greater share of income and wealth from the rapidly expanding trade with Asia and the new world.

The effect of these forces was a dramatic shift in wealth and, therefore, power, in the years leading up to the Civil War. One commentator of the time had noted that, "The House of Commons could buy the House of Lords three times over." Even if overstated, this comment reflected the dramatic reversal of fortunes that had occurred between the two classes over the prior century.

Finally, the Stuart kings of the 1600s were relatively poor, especially compared with the expanding expectations of a monarch in the early seventeenth century. They had trouble getting money from Parliament so used other, extra-Parliamentary means of raising funds. One of these means included the sale of titles—knights; viscounts; barons; dukes, etc.—to wealthy gentry aspiring for higher social status. This had the effect of lowering the prestige of the nobility as a class. So, the military capacity, the wealth, the income, and the social prestige of the nobility of England was shrinking in the years leading up to the Civil War. Rising challengers would turn this to their advantage.

Religious Conflicts

The second fundamental conflict was religious. Henry's Anglican Church was the first state church to separate from Rome. Elizabeth I, Henry's daughter who ruled from 1558 to 1603, managed the tension between traditional Catholicism and newly-formed Anglicanism with an ingenious formula. She kept the outward form of Catholic worship, including its elaborate ceremony and rich iconography, but did not require churchgoers to declare their personal religion. As she is said to have stated, "I have no desire to make windows into men's souls."

This "Elizabethan Settlement" as it came to be known, worked brilliantly, satisfying both Catholics and Protestants. While the European continent was riven with wars of religion in the late 1500s, England enjoyed a half-century of confessional peace.

But Henry's Anglicanism was based on an organizational model supported by Luther in Germany: *cuius regio; eius religio*. This meant "whose realm; his religion." In other words, the reigning prince would determine the religion of his people. (Henry's theologians had consulted directly with Luther in devising Anglicanism.) This produced a "top-down" system of church governance that, in some ways, was not unlike that of the Catholic Church. The Anglican Church was governed by an "episcopacy" of bishops who imposed doctrine and practices from above, much as the strata of cardinals and archbishops did in the Catholic Church.

On the other hand, those Protestant churches that arose later, on the basis of the teachings of John Calvin, an early revisionist of Luther, followed practices where power emerged from below and was more widely dispersed in the congregation. This included the Presbyterian Church, which was popular in Scotland, and the even more egalitarian Puritan practice, which had gained popularity in England. Both Presbyterians and Puritans despised the "popish" Anglicanism with its hierarchical doctrines and its seeming emphasis on outward appearances over inward conviction.

Their hostility was made all the more vehement when, in the 1630s, the Anglican Church embraced the teachings of Jacobus Arminius, a Dutch theologian who had broken with Calvinism. Arminianism brought Anglicanism even closer to Catholicism by rejecting Calvin's core doctrine of predestination. Arminius believed, as did the Catholics, that a person's salvation could not be pre-determined by God, otherwise he would have no capacity for moral choice. The Puritans reacted with literally religious fervor to what they saw as a heretical imposition of "popish" practices and a covert agenda on the part of the king to return England to Catholicism.

This religious issue compounded the economic issues discussed above. The most vibrant sector of English society had embraced Calvinism with its stern work ethic of industriousness, thrift, sobriety, and moral probity. This was the gentry. The more stagnant economic sector of society—the nobility, which mainly earned income from rents—was, not surprisingly, associated with the more traditional and top down Anglicanism.

Political Conflicts

The third fundamental conflict, one tied up with both the religious and economic matters, was political. The issue here was two-fold: whether people had a right to be represented in the government; and who was the best defender of their rights. The view of the king on the first issue was that there was no right of representation. This belief derived from two separate sources.

The first source was the traditional feudal understanding that the crown was private property. The king's exercise of royal privileges was no different than a businessman's. It was a private matter and nobody else's business. Though he might be the executor of common affairs, he was not a trustee of common interests.

The second and more important source of the belief that the people had no right to representation came from the doctrine of the "divine right of kings." The King, according to this view, was God's emissary on earth. James I epitomized this idea when he declared, "Kings are as little Gods on earth." As subjects of "little Gods," the people were bound to obedience.

This doctrine had its origins in the Bible. Romans 13 states, "Let every soul be in subjection to the higher powers...he that resists that power defies the ordinance of God and shall receive unto himself Judgment." Just as God could do no wrong before man, the King could do no wrong before his subjects. Challenges represented not just treason, but heresy. This view held substantial sway when the Bible was an important source of authority. But in an age when Protestantism focused less on church dogma and more on the individual's faith, and when science had begun to usurp the authority of the Bible, it had lost quite a bit of its force.

Moreover, Englishmen had been given rights in 1215 by the Magna Carta. These included the right to freedom from taxation without representation, the right to trial by jury, and the right to be secure in their homes from unwarranted search and seizure. Who would be the defender of these rights—the second of the political issues—would become a central issue provoking the Civil War. The King, as a "little god," claimed he knew best. Parliament claimed that the King had violated the people's rights and was no longer a defender of them. They claimed that it fell to them to speak for and defend the rights of the English people against the abuses of the king.

Thus, with rising economic power and the influence that went along with it, together with the conviction afforded by a new religious fervor, Parliament began to assert its political power as well. As was the case with religion and economics, the Parliamentarians faced off against the monarchists in what became the final and decisive conflict leading to civil war. It was a conflict that would help define the very character of the modern world.

3   Prelude To War

Elizabeth died without an heir in 1603. Hers was a hard act to follow. For almost 50 years, she had held England together against all manner of divisive forces. She had contained the religious division between Protestants and Catholics while much of the continent had descended into religious war. She had kept the country at relative peace with the rest of Europe. She had created a unique unity among different classes in English society and between the Crown and Parliament. And she had overseen a remarkable economic prosperity in which all Englishmen shared. She was widely loved and almost universally admired. It is no exaggeration to state that her reign was a "Golden Age," one never surpassed and perhaps never equaled.

James I

Her successor, James I of the Stuart family, was no Elizabeth. He was from Scotland, the son of the Catholic Mary Queen of Scots. He was self-righteous, intolerant, vain, coarse, opinionated, and a zealous believer in the divine right of kings. In 1597 he had written a book, "The Trew Law of Free Monarchies," in which he wrote,

> *"Kings arose before any estates or ranks of men, before any parliaments…And so it follows of necessity that kings were the authors and makers of the laws, and not the laws of the kings."*

He had also written to his son concerning this right:

> *"Just as no misconduct on the part of a father can free his children from obedience, so no misgovernment on the part of a King can release his subjects from their allegiance."*

None of this endeared him to the English people who accepted his ascension to the throne with trepidation.

Perhaps his worst failing was that while he had little money of his own, he was a lavish spender of other people's money, demanding it and sometimes coercing it. This caused him to clash repeatedly with Parliament from which he constantly demanded money. When Parliament would not grant him money, he sold monopolies—the right of a single business to control trade in critical goods, for example, sugar, soap, or salt—to supporters of the crown. This angered the common people who had to pay higher prices for essential commodities, and it enraged merchants whose competing businesses were damaged.

Just after his ascension to the throne, Charles married a Catholic princess from France, the Bourbon Henrietta Maria. This left people suspicious about his intentions for the rest of the country. Parliament wrote to him, saying, "There is a general fear among your people of some secret working to change our holy religion." This fear was not entirely unfounded as Maria openly practiced Catholicism in violation (some said contempt) of the rule of the land which held Anglicanism as the official state church. Charles was also the first king since the Reformation to receive an official emissary from the Pope. More significantly, several of the highest officials of the King's cabinet, including the Lord of the Treasury, the Chancellor of the Exchequer, and the Secretary of State were avowed Catholics.

Most provocatively, Charles elevated William Laud to the position of Archbishop of Canterbury, chief ecclesiastic of the Church of England. Laud espoused Arminianism which was even closer to Catholicism than was Anglicanism. Arminianism held that there was no predestination, a core tenet of most Protestant faiths. Moreover, in Arminianism salvation is available to all, not just to the "saved and elect" as Calvin had taught. It is dependent only on man's exercise of free will. Laud's Arminian innovations reduced the role of lay preaching in the church and elevated the central role of communion. It increased the importance of iconography and religious ceremony and reinstated the role of bishops in overseeing local religious practice.

Many of these innovations reflected policies that the Catholic Church had approved at the Council of Trent in 1565. As such, they were abhorred by most Protestants, and especially Puritans who strove to practice the "pure" Christianity of their belief. The suspicion seemed inescapable that Charles was intent on forcing a thinly disguised Catholicism on the people. The effect was to inflame the people who reacted violently to the "popish plots" of their king.

In 1637, Charles, through Laud, tried to impose the Arminian-influenced Anglican prayer book on Presbyterian Scotland—a move that provoked violent reaction among the Scots. In 1639, Charles raised a small army to confront the Scots but was defeated in 1640, with the result that the Scots occupied Northumberland in northern England. He hadn't enough money or men to win what was called the Bishop's War. He needed Parliament to provide both. But he had lost all sympathy from Parliament for dismissing it 11 years earlier.

When Charles finally recalled Parliament in 1640 to request the funds, it was in no mood to be gracious. During the period of Personal Rule, Charles had imposed a tax to help defend the nation's coastlines, the infamous "ship tax." But he had done so without consent of Parliament, a violation of his own pledge in the *Petition of Right*. And Charles' war against Scotland had been undertaken without consulting

Parliament either, the first time that had been done since 1323. In response, Parliament made other assertions of power that went to the heart of "The Royal Prerogative."

Among such claims, Parliament asserted its right to meet at least every three years, whether the king agreed or not. It claimed that it could not be dismissed by the king, only by its own action. It claimed, as had the *Petition of Right*, that the king could not impose taxes without Parliament's consent. And it asserted a say in the appointment of the king's ministers. All of these claims to Legislative rights would later be embodied in the U.S. Constitution. In another fit of pique, Charles dismissed Parliament again, after it had sat for only three weeks. This earned the body the notorious name, "The Short Parliament."

The situation became even more dire in 1641 when the Catholic Irish rebelled against persecution at the hands of the Protestant English. Relations between Charles and Parliament had become so strained that even as Englishmen in Ireland were being slaughtered, Parliament would not vote the money for Charles to raise an army and defend the country. They were worried—not without reasonable suspicion—that once the rebellion was put down, an army under Charles' control would be turned against them.

By late 1641, riots protesting the king's actions had begun to break out in London. These partly reflected dire economic circumstances that had befallen the country. And they gave specific voice to suspicions that "papists" were in control of the government. Passions were inflamed further by Parliament's issuance of a *Grand Remonstrance* rebuking the actions of the king in religious, financial, judicial, military, and foreign affairs. Parliament, led by the virulently anti-Catholic Puritan, John Pym, played up all of these grievances with the effect that London became polarized between increasingly unyielding religious and political partisans.

In January, 1642, with chaos erupting on all sides and completely unable to govern, Charles moved his royal offices out of London to Oxford. He began to raise his own army to march against Parliament and raised his royal banner in Nottingham in August of that year. It was an effective declaration of war. Thus began the English Civil War.

4 The Civil War

The Civil War began reluctantly. Parliament was still a conservative institution, ruled as it was by a noble-dominated House of Lords, and a gentry-dominated House of Commons. They both respected tradition (though the Commons, perhaps somewhat less) and feared the devastation that would attend a civil war. A civil war would pit almost all parts of English society against some other. Indeed, Ireland divided into Royalists, Catholics, and Parliamentarians. In Scotland, the Presbyterians fell against the Royalists.

England itself was an even more incoherent mess: Royalists against Parliamentarians, Anglicans against Puritans, Nobility against Gentry, court against country. It was what the political philosopher Thomas Hobbes would later describe in *Leviathan* as "a war of all against all."

In all of this, however, Charles was unable to raise an effective army to prosecute the Royalist cause. This was understandable given the conflicts and events that had led up to the War. Merchants hated

Charles for his forced loans, monopolies, and his taxes on ships. The common people hated him for imposing local rule by the Anglican clergy and for raising taxes on essential foodstuffs. The Scots hated him for persecuting Presbyterians and the Irish hated him for not protecting Catholics. Except for the increasingly ineffectual nobility, some of whom had already defected in protest of Charles' imperiousness, and those who were simply sentimentally loyal to monarchy, Charles was largely friendless.

It is no surprise, therefore, that Charles' defense of his crown failed. Fighting started in 1642 and continued for three more years. Charles' troops fought from the sparsely populated countryside against the more densely populated urban areas. They constantly lacked money and war-fighting materials. They were short of manpower and when they did win, it was largely because their Parliamentary-led opposition really had no heart for fighting their own king. Charles himself was chased from one county to another, often in disguise, frequently slipping out of hiding places just ahead of his pursuers. It was a pathetic performance, diminishing the very office of the king itself.

The opposition rallied under the leadership of a Scottish Puritan, Oliver Cromwell. Cromwell had been a member of the House of Commons since 1628, the year the *Petition of Right* was signed. He was an imposing leader and proved himself a brilliant battle-field commander. Cromwell formed a "New Model Army" that was known as the "Roundheads."

The Roundheads, largely populated by evangelical Puritans, believed that God had anointed the war a battle for a "New Jerusalem," a conflict described in the Bible to signify the return of Christ to earth and the imposition of a second Kingdom of Heaven. They fought with religious fervor and decisively defeated Charles' Royalist army, the "Cavaliers," in 1644 at the Battle of Marston Moor. Cromwell and his Roundheads finished off the Cavaliers at the Battle of Naseby in 1645. Charles was defeated, captured and put under house arrest in 1646.

The next two years involved a protracted negotiation between Charles and the Parliamentarians led by Cromwell. The negotiations concerned an important question: on what terms might the king serve? Would it be a return to divine right with all the contempt of the Parliament and a "popish" religious establishment that that doctrine implied? Or would it be a collaborative rule in partnership with Parliament which was dominated by Presbyterians and Puritans with their more egalitarian ethic?

On the political part of this question, Charles was unyielding. He would *never* submit to partnership with a body (Parliament) that he viewed as profane and constricting his "divine right" to rule. Ironically, the Parliamentarians *wanted* a king but would not abide one who could barely acknowledge their right to exist. Charles escaped house arrest in 1648 and mounted a brief but futile effort to recapture the government. This "Second Civil War" was quickly put down by Cromwell who now realized the country would never be at peace so long as Charles was still alive.

5 The Trial and Execution of Charles I

In January 1649, out of more than 300 members of Parliament, Oliver Cromwell chose 46 to be jurors in the trial of Charles Stuart. Members who might have been sympathetic to Charles' position were excluded. In other words, the trial was rigged, and everyone knew it. Cromwell wanted a veneer of legitimacy for the trial, but even more than that, he wanted a verdict that would condemn Charles to death.

The trial highlighted the extremes between Charles' vision of a king's rights and the Parliament's vision of what powers a king might have. Charles was charged with trying to carry out "a wicked design to erect and uphold in himself an unlimited and tyrannical power to rule according to his will, and to overthrow the rights and liberties of the people of England." When asked how he pleaded in response to the charges, including those of being "a Tyrant, a Traitor, a Murderer, and a public Enemy to the Commonwealth of England," Charles refused to answer, replying instead, greater interests of the people as expressed through Parliament. That is the transitional fulcrum on which the entire affair rose and fell.

The secondary point is the inescapable necessity of cooperation between executive and legislature and, implicitly, the equality of the legislature with the king. Charles would not abide either of these interpretations of the emerging principles of constitutionalism and representation. He fully believed he had been placed on the throne by God and that to equivocate with Parliament in the discharge of his duties would be a sin against God.

Charles was condemned to death but remained defiant to the end. On the scaffold, as he was about to be put to death, he made the following statement:

> *"I shall begin first with my innocence…all the world knows I never did begin a war with the two Houses of Parliament. I never did encroach upon their privileges. They began upon mine. They confessed that the Militia was mine but they thought it fit for to have it from me…*
>
> *Now for to show you that I am a good Christian. I have forgiven all the world, and even those in particular that have been the chief causes of my death…I pray God that this [act] be not laid to their charge, for my charity commands me to forgive not only particular men, but to endeavor to the last gasp the Peace of the Kingdom…*

*For the people, truly I desire their liberty and
freedom as much as anybody. But I must tell you
that their liberty and freedom consists in having a
government and laws by which their life and their
goods may be most their own. It is not for having a
share in government. That is nothing pertaining
to them. A subject and a sovereign are clear
different things…*

*It was for this that I am come here. I have delivered
my conscience. I pray God that you do take those
courses that are best for the good of the Kingdom
and your own salvations."*

His head was cut off on January 30, 1649. To the
end, Charles asserted the medieval concept of the
crown as the private purview of the king. He also
asserted his role in protecting the liberties of the
English people against the legal inventions of the
Parliament. In overthrowing him, Parliament asserted
a contrary vision: that the state was the purview of
all the people; that their right to participation in its
governance could not be abridged; that all people
were entitled to the protection of the Law; and that it
was the place of Parliament to ensure that violations
of the law against the interests of the people were not
allowed.

The War and Charles' overthrow represented,
therefore, an epochal turning point in the evolution
of political affairs in the Western world. It was the
first time in the history of the Western world that a

sitting monarch was executed by a rebellion of his own people. The office of King and the House of Lords were abolished the following month and England began its experiment of creating a new form of government out of the shattered remnants of the old.

6 The Interregnum

Having won the Civil War and with the power of the army behind him, Oliver Cromwell became the head of government. He wanted Parliamentary rule and made many concessions to balance the power of the Executive with that of the Legislative branch. For example, he created a Council of State composed of ministers who would act as an Executive branch. This was balanced by a 400 member Parliament acting as the Legislative branch. He agreed that major decisions of the Executive should be subject to the approval of the Legislature. This foreshadowed the right of veto and override in the U.S. Constitution.

However, religious hostility, a recurrent theme both before and during the War, remained. Cromwell was a devout Puritan and intended to use his new position to impose his religious views on the government. So, when the new Council of State was convened, Cromwell said to them at their first meeting,

"Truly, you are called by God to rule with Him, and for Him. And you are called to be faithful with the Saints, who have been somewhat instrumental in your call... Jesus Christ is owned this day by your call; and you own Him by your willingness to appear for Him."

Cromwell held an abiding hatred of the Catholic Church. He led an invasion of Ireland in 1649 to suppress the Irish revolt. Resistance was fierce. Over 10,000 Irishmen, mostly Catholics, including women, children, and priests, were killed. Some 12,000 people were sold by the government into slavery. Catholic lands were confiscated and given to Protestant English settlers, and the open practice of communion was outlawed.

Cromwell completed a similar conquest of Scotland by 1655, though without the wholesale slaughter or the expropriation of Scottish lands. Presbyterianism was allowed to be practiced, but the church was forbidden to issue judicial rulings as it had done before the War.

Cromwell arranged for both Scotland and Ireland to be represented in Parliament, the first time that had ever happened. Cromwell gave himself the title of Lord Protector but declined the position of king when it was urged on him by the Parliament, declaring, "I would not seek to set up that which Providence hath destroyed and laid in the dust." But despite his anti-monarchical inclinations Cromwell was equally intent that Parliamentary rule should not violate religious toleration for Protestants. When, in 1653, Parliament passed legislation increasing persecution of religious minorities, Cromwell had it dissolved, ironically exhibiting the same imperiousness that he had condemned Charles for.

The question of how to rule without a king (England had not been without a king for over a thousand years) was complicated by the intense religious factionalism that now tore at the Parliament. At one extreme were the relatively wealthy Presbyterians who wanted to run the government along the lines of their Scottish religion but who wanted no other changes to the social order, certainly not any that might threaten property. At the other extreme were the relatively poor Puritans who wanted to completely undo existing social relations, abolish private property, and give all males the right to vote.

In the middle were the Independents led by Cromwell and backed by the New Model Army. Unlike the Presbyterians who wanted strict religious uniformity throughout the kingdom, Cromwell wanted liberty of conscience, so long as it was not a Catholic conscience. But he was closer to the Presbyterians on economic and social matters. Where the Puritans leaned toward social leveling, Cromwell, as a country gentlemen of some means, favored retention of social hierarchy as a means of maintaining public order. The turbulence that arose from these conflicting tendencies tore not only at Parliament but at the country as a whole.

7   The Restoration

By 1660, the English people were fatigued from 20 years of civil war and governmental upheaval. Despite the many failings of monarchy, the experiment in popular rule had proven even worse, plunging the country into little more than a police state. The hostilities of Englishman against Englishman drained the people's energies. And, government affairs had become frozen at precisely the time that the English had begun to challenge the Dutch for global commercial supremacy. Decisive leadership was needed, but leadership that brought the people together, that united them under a single national identity and mission. The English people wanted their king back.

Charles II

Since the beginning of the War, Charles' son, Charles II, had been in exile in France. He had learned from his father's experience the lessons of being too rigid in defiance of Parliament. And so, he made soothing overtures toward Parliament regarding his acceptance of its role in English governance. He also spoke of his desire that Englishmen should enjoy "liberty of conscience," a clear reference to the religious dimension of the Civil War. Warmed by these assurances, Parliament, in 1660, invited Charles to return to England to restore the Stuart monarchy. He returned, was met with a buoyant reception, and was crowned King Charles II in 1661.

But many of the conflicts that had motivated the War in the first place—the right of succession, the right to call and dismiss Parliament, religious rights— had never really been resolved and were only swept under the carpet in the euphoria of Restoration. They would eventually come back to haunt the country. Religion, of course, was one of the most central of these conflicts.

Charles continued his family's affinity with Catholicism. He made a secret deal with Louis XIV, king of France, to convert England back to Catholicism once the timing was right. In exchange, he received secret subsidies from Louis. His younger brother, James, married a Catholic, upsetting Charles' English subjects because Charles was without heirs so James was next in line to the throne. Wisely, Charles balanced his preference for Catholicism by appointing Protestants to important ministerial posts.

Remarkably, finances were not a pressing issue for the King and so did not incite the hostilities they had during the reign of Charles' father. In addition to the allotment from Parliament and its secret subsidies from France, the Crown benefited from a spectacular expansion of British commerce that flooded the treasury with tax revenues. As long as the economy was strong and everybody was getting richer, Charles' dalliances with Catholicism were tolerated. Charles died in 1685 and was succeeded by his younger brother, James.

James II

Unlike Charles II who had moderated his religious preferences out of respect (or fear) of Parliament, James was an unapologetic Catholic. Where Charles had been cautious, James was now brazen. He dismissed Charles' Protestant ministers, bishops, and civil servants and replaced them with Catholics. He similarly vacated the largely-Protestant officer corps of the army, and packed it with loyal Catholics as well. But since there were relatively few Catholics in England by this time, the people he chose were mediocre, never earning the respect of those they were appointed to lead. This move cost him the loyalty of many members of the nobility, members who would have tolerated him otherwise.

More important, James' wholesale appointment of Catholics provoked Parliament to pass a law prohibiting Catholics from serving in public positions. Once again, a religious confrontation had become the impetus for Parliament increasing its authority at the expense of the king's. When Parliament asked James to enforce the laws against "all dissenters from

invasion force of 400 ships to carry 60,000 soldiers and 5,000 horses for an invasion of England. Louis XIV learned of the planned invasion and threatened Holland but he was mired in battles elsewhere and in the end did not interfere.

The invasion was delayed by several weeks of bad weather, making it difficult for the ships to leave from Dutch ports. But once underway, it went off flawlessly, facing virtually no opposition from either the English people or the army. The English navy switched loyalties and fell in behind William. So too did many nobles, leaving James isolated and powerless. To avoid a stain on his imminent kingship (and out of deference to Mary, his wife and James' daughter), William allowed James to slip quietly out of the country to France, effectively abdicating the throne and leaving it open to his own ascension.

This "Glorious Revolution," as it came to be called, was the last foreign invasion of England, an effective *coup d'etat*. It put a final end to questions of Catholicism as a state church. It also ended the pretensions to absolute rule that had also begun with James I. It symbolized, as no other event could, the extent to which Parliamentary power had grown over the preceding century, even surpassing that of the king. Far from its lowly status when it sat only at the pleasure of the king, Parliament was now the body that made and unmade the king. It was a titanic shift, literally unimaginable only 50 years before.

Moreover, Parliament's offer to William was not without important conditions. Before it acceded to his ascension, it insisted that he agree to a Bill of Rights, which was signed in 1689. This historic document guaranteed Englishmen the protection in law that Parliament had fought so vigorously for. It specifically forbade the king from abolishing laws passed by Parliament. Neither could he levy taxes unilaterally, as Charles I had done. Nor could he maintain a standing army in peacetime as Cromwell had done.

Finally, the Act of Toleration that followed the Bill of Rights guaranteed religious toleration to all Protestants but specifically forbade succession to the English throne by a Catholic. Over the next two decades, these limitations on the monarchy were extended still further, thus instituting the first limited constitutional monarchy in the modern world.

9 Reflections on the Founding of America

The 1600s was a remarkable century in England. In politics, Parliamentary government emerged from the dominating shadow of Monarchy to create a new, balanced form of government where Parliament and king were co-equals. In legal matters, constitutionalism replaced absolutism. In religious affairs, Catholicism was permanently banned from the English monarchy while intolerance and persecution gave way to acceptance and protection—at least for Protestants. And in the economic arena, the landed nobility of feudal times declined while the merchant class of a nascent capitalism expanded in size and grew in power.

It is impossible to overstate how important these changes were to the growing English colonies in the New World. America was, after all, largely an English creation and its citizens were mainly from England. New York is called *New* York because there is an *old* York in England. Similarly, there is an *old* Jersey and an *old* Hampshire in England as well. Georgia, Virginia,

1629	Charles dismisses Parliament; begins 11 years of Personal Rule
1637	Charles tries to force Anglican prayer book on Scotland; rebellion breaks out
1640	Charles recalls Parliament to seek funds to prosecute Bishop's War
1641	Irish Rebellion breaks out; Charles requests army from Parliament but is denied
1642	Charles moves to Oxford; English Civil War begins
1644	Royalist "Cavalier" army defeated at Marston Moor
1645	Royalist "Cavalier" army decisively defeated at Naseby
1646	Charles taken prisoner; Oliver Cromwell assumes control of Parliament
1648	Charles escapes and begins second Civil War; is captured and returned to captivity
1649	Charles is beheaded; monarchy and House of Lords are abolished

Begin Interregnum

1649   Cromwell suppresses Leveller mutiny in the army and Catholic rebellion in Ireland

1651   First Navigation Act; English trade must be carried on English ships

1654   Cromwell dissolves Parliament, institutes martial law

1658   Oliver Cromwell dies

End Interregnum

1661   Charles II assumes throne in Restoration

1685   Charles II dies; his brother, James II, ascends to throne

1688   James II abdicates; William and Mary assume throne in Glorious Revolution

1689   English Bill of Rights enacted

1763   End of Seven Years (French and Indian) War between England and France

           King George begins raising taxes to repay debts run up during the War

1773   Boston Tea Party; colonists protest unilateral imposition of taxes without representation

1776	Englishman Thomas Jefferson writes the Declaration of Independence
1787	Former Englishman James Madison writes the American Constitution; adopted in 1789
1789	Former Englishman George Mason writes the American Bill of Rights; adopted in 1791

If you enjoyed this book, please look for all of the titles in *The Best One-Hour History* series.

- Ancient Greece
- Rome
- The Middle Ages
- The Renaissance
- The Protestant Reformation
- European Wars of Religion
- The English Civil Wars
- The Scientific Revolution
- The Enlightenment
- The American Revolution
- The French Revolution
- The Industrial Revolution
- Europe in the 1800s
- The American Civil War
- European Imperialism
- World War I
- The Interwar Years
- World War II
- The Cold War
- The Vietnam War

To learn more about each title and its expected publication date, visit: *http://onehourhistory.com*

CPSIA information can be obtained at www.ICGtesting.com
Printed in the USA
LVOW04s0446090915

453287LV00033BA/1597/P